PRAISE FOʀ *HAPPY, OKAY?*

"*M.J. Fievre's* Happy, Okay? *offers us a hybrid reading experience. In this poem-play, or play-poem 'a shadow/woman, a charcoal sketch' journeys through the labyrinth of Big Pharma, a difficult love affair, and self-reflection to reach moments of the divine. Though hopeful,* Happy, Okay? *is not a happily-ever-after tale, but a realistic look at mental illness, the patriarchy, race, and gender. M.J. Fievre beautifully conjures a complex inner life under Miami's glaring sun.*"

—**Denise Duhamel**, National Endowment for the Arts Fellow, and guest editor of *The Best American Poetry 2013*

"Happy, Okay? *is a beautifully written meditation filled with poignant and lyrical revelations on the joys, pains, and complications of life and the daily struggle to survive, create, and love.*"

—**Edwidge Danticat**, internationally acclaimed Haitian-American novelist and short story writer

"*M.J. Fievre has written a classic Greek drama set in Hialeah, a latticework of speech set, at first, on the stage of a Metrorail station, and then in the manifesto-ridden psyche of a Miami woman in the midst of a rebirth. And what's more Miami than a*

reinvention? The story in Happy, Okay? is timeless—
love gained, love lost—but the characters and setting
are pure Miami. My heart leapt every time I came
across a mamey, an azalea, or a sapote. I could
hear the rara band. I could taste the cold bottle of
Prestige. 'Where we come from,' Fievre writes, 'no
one has the luxury of self-loathing.' This isn't the
Miami you read about in brochures; it's the Miami
where 'the moon is throwing knives through the
trees;' 'Coqui frogs sing their love-croaks;' and the
air smells like breadfruit. In other words, it's the
Miami we love."

—**Scott Cunningham**, founder/executive director of
O, Miami

"M.J. Fievre's poem, Happy, Okay? is an ambitious,
fascinating, sprawling, multivoiced work that sucks
the reader in and does not let go. In rhythmic,
evocative poetry, Fievre brings to vivid life the
story of Paloma and Jose Armando—with Shadow, a
disembodied voice of pain and hurt, swirling around
them and within them. In Fievre's lines, the city of
Miami, specifically its Hialeah neighborhood, becomes
more than just the backdrop for these two lovers—in
Happy, Okay? we hear and sense the sounds, sights,
and languages, the patois of Haitians, Jamaicans, and
Cubans, the sweetness of tropical fruit. These lovers
orbit each other in their pain and desire, but the
reader will soon discover this is no mere tale of ill-
fated lovers. It's a meditation on what we need to be
happy, and an exploration of that hard-won wisdom.
This poem, this book, will both haunt and delight,

tease and deliver. It's a world of wonder, and a salve for our troubled times."

—**Allison Joseph**, author of *Confessions of a Barefaced Woman*

"In Paloma, M.J. Fievre has created a woman struggling for self-discovery. This is not easy when Paloma knows all too well that at the borders of existence dwell darkness, depression, and dead-eyed grief. A place where love can be both oasis and razor; where affection can become a ghostly and fleeting affliction not easily healed by words or human touch. Paloma travels these borderlands—far beyond grim silences and all-consuming shadows; far beyond medications like Zoloft, Prozac, & Luvox that have comprised the lexicon of her human imbalance to ultimately reach the true north of human love. Love of self, and love of others. Ultimately, it is through Paloma's journey that we can all learn to heal—if we remember to breathe, practice gratitude, and self-care. And above all else, keep the faith."

—**Rich Ferguson**, LA poet/novelist/spoken-word performer

"M.J. Fievre's Happy, Okay? is a healing balm, a rapturous song of the self, a reminder that breaking is just another kind of rebirth. Told in breathtaking monologues and poetry, Happy, Okay? examines the roles we wear and let loose, and the stories we hold in our shadows. This collection declares 'You are here. Nowhere else. & you are divine.' A must read!

You'll be happy you picked up Happy, Okay? *and happy to share it with everyone you know."*

—Jennifer Maritza McCauley, author of *SCAR ON/ SCAR OFF*

"Think of this beautiful book as a toolkit of verse shedding light on what it's like, what it's really like, to suffer from, or love someone suffering from, anxiety and mental illness. A musical weapon of a fable for girls of all colors, so that they may manage a confusing world and save themselves with self-love."

—Anjanette Delgado, author of *The Clairvoyant of Calle Ocho*

"Clinical depression is a cold hand squeezing your heart. Anxiety feels like a close call with death. Reading Happy, Okay? *told me I'm not alone in the struggle with mental illness. Paloma, the protagonist, goes from drowning in a sea of hopelessness to swimming to the shore of joy, deftly sharing with the reader tools to navigate the murky waters of her brain. In the end, happiness requires some work from within. I know it first-hand. On reading M.J. Fievre's narrative poem, I believe the reader will know too."*

—Lorraine C. Ladish, founder of VivaFifty.com & TheFlawedYogini.com

"In this brave and complex narrative poem, M. J. Fievre rips the veil from the face of mental illness, showing us a tortured emotional landscape that disavows the salvific potential of romance and eschews easy notions of escape from a mind inured in pain. Paloma, the female speaker in the poem, is keenly aware of the maelstrom of chaos, indeterminacy, and fragility that renders her internal landscape a site of trauma that will require therapy, medication, time, and interiority to restore.

*"*Happy, Okay? *uses language that is raw, fresh, and at times, startling beautiful, to chart a myriad existence that recalls and implicates personal and political history, memory, home, family, and lived experience as sites of alterity, sustenance, alienation and possibility.*

"Place is paramount in Fievre's poem. Miami, the northernmost Caribbean city, is a uniquely American polyglot of Haitian Creole, Jamaican Patois, Cuban Spanish, cortaditos and café-crème. Rendered as co-conspirator in the trauma of erasure for the Black Caribbean female subject, Miami is also a site of reconstitution and re-memory.

Miami is a conspiracy of ravens
on telephone poles. Miami is roads
always under construction...

"The Caribbean, a priori site of alterity, liminality and displacement, is also home. But it is a home that incites psychic and existential homelessness, silences and erasures with its disquieting and irreconcilable contradictions.

"Yet Paloma, while brutally honest, is never hopeless. Clear-eyed and unsentimental, she disavows facile notions of wholeness and unity in a world that fragments, displaces and discards with impunity. If she has one salvific wish, it is the wish to be her own messiah. She is fragile, yet stubbornly determined to name, define, dissect, and thereby claim ownership and authority over her depression, sedulously reaching for stability and empowerment via the aegis of audacious storytelling, rigorous self-excavation and emerging faith."

—**Donna Aza Weir-Soley**, author of *Eroticism, Spirituality, and Resistance in Black Women's Writings* and *The Woman Who Knew*

"*Every sentence is ripe with flourish.*"

—**The Miami Herald**

"*She writes masterfully of emotion, giving concrete weight to words that are otherwise just floating, fluttering ideas.*"

—**Pank Magazine**

"*A fresh voice in an increasingly globalized world, MJ is well on her way to becoming one of our generations' most enduring literary talents.*"

—**Saw Palm: Florida Literature & Art**

Happy, Okay?

Happy, Okay?

POEMS ABOUT ANXIETY,
DEPRESSION, HOPE, & SURVIVAL

M.J. FIEVRE

Mango Publishing
CORAL GABLES

For permission requests, please contact the publisher at:
Mango Publishing Group
2850 S Douglas Road, 2nd Floor
Coral Gables, FL 33134 USA
info@mango.bz

For special orders, quantity sales, course adoptions and corporate sales, please email the publisher at sales@mango.bz. For trade and wholesale sales, please contact Ingram Publisher Services at customer.service@ingramcontent.com or +1.800.509.4887.

Happy, Okay?: Poems about Anxiety, Depression, Hope, & Survival

Library of Congress Cataloging-in-Publication number: 2019948828
ISBN: (p) 978-1-64250-136-0 (e) 978-1-64250-137-7
BISAC category code POETRY / Subjects & Themes / Death, Grief, Loss

Printed in the United States of America

To my husband Thomas,
I love the woman I am with you

Paloma, José Armando's lover
José Armando, Paloma's lover
Shadow, a shadowy character

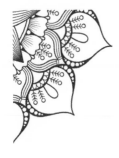
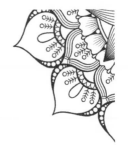

Part 1

Happy, Happy, Joy, Joy

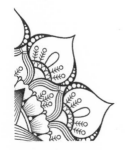
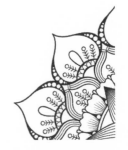

José Armando

It's 75 degrees
at the Metrorail station
in Hialeah,
where girls wait
to be whisked away
in shorts, tank tops
& sandals,
in the South Florida breeze
that rustles their hair.

Others stand
in leather boots & winter
coats—furry
& smooth & clean.

At the mom-&-pop
pancake place,
they will order
in Spanish, Creole,
& Jamaican patois. They
will want French
baguettes, cortaditos
& café-crème.

In the afternoon,
the sky will darken
& someone
with an umbrella
will suggest
a trip to El Rinconcito

on 56th Street.

Paloma,
by the time
I head home,
through the corridors
between the botanica
& the Catholic
store, it will be hot
again—because
Hialeah is very
temperamental.

A bit like you.

Shadow

The faces around you
are unfamiliar, but
the longer you stare,
the less they are
strangers—
your brown eyes / brown
skin in other bodies,
walking the same
streets you've walked since
your feet learned
to hold your body upright.

The shoeshine men set up
a high chair & a table
in front of a café,
which smells of
sweet rolls &
beef patties behind
its closed
doors. They play
dominoes,
their faces frowning,
but a smile
only inches away.
Hands slap
knees when laughter
erupts—volcanic,
stretching
their cheeks under
straw hats.

This new Miami day
is buoyant
like yeasty Cuban bread.
But you've forgotten
the rich, full-throated
sound of your own
laughter.
You've buried it so deep
it resides in your
empty belly
and cannot escape
beyond your throat.

Paloma

I am leaving you,
& in the apartment we shared,
there is nothing left
on the walls
but nails
that held
our engagement
pictures. My bottles
of French perfume
have been packed
away,
leaving their dusty
shapes
on the vanity.

Where the radio used
to sit on the bookshelf,
there's a gap,
like a missing tooth.

I think of old Caribbean men
who stand in the back
at weddings,
their faces creased.
They angle
coins in their pockets
to claim a grasp on calm.
Their eyes go
this way & that
—this way & that.

& the aunties
are fat with thick
whiskers on their chins.
They wear wide-brimmed
hats & dresses in bright
yellows, reds, & whites.

There will be
no wedding for us.
I am leaving you,
& in the apartment we shared,
there is nothing left
on the walls
but nails
that held
our engagement
pictures. Everything
I own has been hauled
back to my childhood
home.

José Armando

For days now,
she's worn
a stranger's face
—tight, unreadable.
& now she's leaving.

I don't want her to go.

Shadow

Yesterday,
everything was bedrock,
determined & solid.
You gripped
each other's hands firmly,
surrounded
by leaves in shades
of green, yellow, red. You
promised
to love
each other
—until the kingdom,
until the power
& the glory,
until the Amen.

& today: this.

She wants to throw
something. But
she doesn't want
that thing to break.
Every now & then,
she feels flashes
of strangeness.
It's like lightning
in the night,
when suddenly
the world turns bright

& the harsh positions
of objects are revealed.

José Armando

Every time
she leaves me,
she packs
all my metaphors
in a torn
suitcase—all my cadences
& hyperboles,
even the syllables
of my own name.
I am left only
with a thick,
heightened
silence,
an absence
of verb.
I can no longer
write about what used
to be, about what is,
& all the future
holds out to me
in promises
is the blur of hot
breath & the howling
in my chest that can't
make its way
through my throat.
My torment
cannot be
translated into
anaphora & dissonance.

Every time
you leave me,
dark things crowd
me: they don't follow
you into the Metro after
your composed goodbyes
& well-behaved tears:
they yell
& make accusations:
they no longer
speak in stanzas
& pentameters: they move
in pangs, shakes,
little tiny heartbreaks
imploding
my ribcage, quick
tides of ache,
& moonless sleeps.
My twisted body
feels its every knot.
In my veins:
pure chaos.

Every time
you leave me,
I am legion
—until the sun rises
or doesn't, until the harsh
light of the day moves
like a slow rolling
stone over the sky.

I want to make you
happy, okay?

Paloma

Every time I return
from the therapist's office,
I walk around with letters
in my head. Imagined
but not composed,
composed but not addressed,
addressed but undelivered,
delivered but unopened,
opened but unread,
read but misunderstood,
& then I'm writing
another letter
& another.
All of them
about break-ups.

Shadow

Without her,
you are the awful quiet
of morning, before
the first train leaves
its depot for the day. Without
her, there is no direction.
Nothing
sweet & succulent
like ripe mamey, warm
from the summer heat.

A man who cannot
light his own fire
is doomed
to reside in only dark
& cold places.
All around you,
the sky is warming
the asphalt; the air is alive.

Paloma

Say something.

José Armando

You scare me
　　when you let yourself
　　　　feel the friction
　　　　　　of open space,
　　　　feel the weight
　　　　　　of too much
　　　　　　　　of nothing,
　　　　　　of

　　　　　　　who
　　　　　　　what
　　　　　　　why
　　　　　　　when.
It all
　　hangs heavy
　　　　on you,
　　drags you down.

You scare me
　　—but I am still here.

Paloma

Every night, the pills
stick in my throat and
work my gag reflex;
I can feel my epiglottis
shift when I swallow.

You watch me
like I'm somebody
who needs watching
& I don't feel beautiful
when I'm pinned
& wriggling
under the microscope
of your gaze.

Instead of medication,
I want sunshine
& birdsongs
—the kind of laughter
that begins in my chest
& tumbles
out & across
my frame like waves
lapping at the shore of a beach.

With or without you
I'm a shadow
woman, a charcoal sketch:
the sky gray,
the earth black,

the trees laced together
by a meshwork of dark
netting. Alone,
even when surrounded.

José Armando

I don't want
to let you go.
When you're furious
at me for no good
reason, recalibrating
a new set of imagined
threats,
I want to keep you
close to me
& hold your cheeks.

So many times
you've worried
me, I've found you
with deep grooves
carved under
your eyes,
your body flat against
the kitchen floor, as if
begging
it for the mercy
of an embrace.

You pine for solitude,
but you have never
been as alone
as when you walk away
from me.

You've left me
a dozen times, & still
come back
for nights
when we walk
beside the moonlit
lake. In the morning,
we watch the sky
turn orange
& azaleas seize
the sunlight.
The late
acacia has tossed
its pollen.
In a few months,
outside the North Hialeah
Baptist Church,
the black sapotes
will be bleeding.
I want to taste
sun-ripened fruit
with you.

If you ever say
you don't believe
in my love:
I'll stretch my arms.
As your muscles
tense against mine—

I will hold you.

From now on, each
time you threaten
to go—far, far away,
never to come back
—I'll pull you close
& allay all your old,
fierce fears,
your deep-rooted
& still-gestating worries.

I waited
for someone
my whole life;
then here you are.
I found you.
I want to see you,
hear you,
smell you,
hold you,
in this space
that belongs
to no one really
—a space of consistent
fluctuation,
a no-man's land
of intimacy.

When you are happy,
it is like the sky
has a new name
that we share.

Let me love you
with a love
so strong it will
propel you
out of your body.

Paloma

You're already
a ghost,
a stranger
in the making.
What was it
we wanted?
What were we
looking for?
I ache
for something
to lead me
to militance,
to strength,
to solace;
maybe a manifesto
whose words
will tingle
my bones
& turn me
into something
greater
than myself.
I'm eager
to create
a new world,
to unravel
the knots
that were tied
long ago.

José Armando

If you stay,
I'll remind
you every day
that I love
you. I'll be gentle.
I don't know how
yet, but I'll make you feel
it: that my closeness
is hard & real,
like a smooth stone
you hold
in your hands.

Paloma

I want to stride
with purpose
& direction
towards something
that fills my body
with bones,
something
dense & heavy
like molten gold.
I want my body
to hum inside itself.
& for that
I need to chart
articles
of a faith I can abide in,
composed
of soft sounds,
like a river uncurling
in a course it sets
for itself.

Your words are pretty,
but they don't ring
from within
me. They clang
off-key,
like a bell
that's been dropped
on a hard surface
too many times.

I am ready,
to remember how to laugh
at the littlest things.
Because
when I can hope,
excitement rises
from the back of my neck,
an exquisite
pulse that activates
the nerve endings
in every millimeter
of my flesh.

I am human—mutable.
Nothing
in the world
is otherwise.

Shadow

When you kiss
him, your finger finds
its way inside the curve
of his ear. You've gotten
to know
the feel of his skin,
his scent an outpour.
Your hands roam
the regions
of his skin, but
you've also climbed
under his dermis, invaded
his capillaries, you've ridden
the waves of his veins,
& settled
the left & right
ventricles of his heart.

It won't be a story
with a good ending.
Something
in his chest
will tear apart
—something
grown over,
tangled,
uncared for.

There's no ointment
for heartache.

No pill for lovelorn.

Every time
you leave him,
silence swallows
the apartment you shared
& he's suspended
in the dark
warmth of its throat.

Paloma

He doesn't know me,
doesn't know
what I'm capable of.
I am a stranger
to myself.
The face
that stares back
from the morning mirror
is a blank canvas
of possibility.

For too many years,
I've allowed others
to hold a paintbrush
and splatter their
images across
its surface. It is time
for me
to dip my own
brush into a palette.
More depth
and shallow,
more dapple of light.
More realism
than impression.

José Armando

Oh, how little it takes
to love her!
The way she says
my name. How she laughs
& wrinkles her forehead after
she's uttered something
strange.

That's what
you do to me:
permeate, saturate,
submerge me
in you.
I love you more
than a person ought
to love one thing.

I want to loosen the knot
between your brows & find
the soft place
within you:
It's there
—somewhere.
I can see it
in the margins
of your eyelashes.

Paloma

Until I find myself,
I am nothing but a buoy,
tied in the calm water,
just beyond
the breaking waves,
far enough
offshore
that I'll never crash
against anything solid,
but just close enough
that I can see a horizon
of blue meeting blue,
ocean & sky,
& I am trapped
in-between,
unable to move
towards depths
nor towards shallows.

Shadow

It is time
you
let her go.
You cannot
hold back
a river forging
a new map
after a flood.
You've grown skillful
at reading the many
browns of her eyes,
& the slight changes
of her voice. One moment,
she smiles
& laughs;
she is composed,
in control, reliable;
the next she is unglued
—a wild-eyed stranger,
& everything
becomes dead eyes
& distance.
You find her
in bed
in the middle
of the afternoon, or
she sits
for hours at a time
on the closed
lid of the toilet, drinking

cheap Manischewitz wine
from a pink Miami
mug. Sometimes,
you find her
standing
in the middle
of the yard, in the pouring
rain, just staring, still
as stone, saying
she wants
to leave you.
For how much longer
do you want her face
to remain your barometer,
your instrument for peace?

José Armando

When sorrow
knocks
on your door,
do you really have
to answer
& kiss the emptiness
—sweet, sour, bitter?

Paloma

You think
I choose
to be this way.

I'll never be someone
with an easy
laugh. I'm lucky
to still be alive.
So many times
I've wanted to hang
myself from the shower rod,
with the rhinestone belt
you gave me
for Christmas
looped
around my neck.
I've imagined it all:
how you'd see me
in the mirror.
I'd hang
in another dimension,
out of anyone's reach,
a reverse world
where anti-matter
ranges free.
That kind of freedom
would be a blessing
sweeter than any kisses
that ever
fell from your mouth.

There are so many
ways to die,
none of them
delicate blossoms.

There are sinister
possibilities
in the most ordinary
items:
kitchen knives
with slight curves, perfect
for mincing & toy swords
& jump ropes
—things that cannot
be captured
by the longing
to be something other
than what they are,
to be somewhere other
than where they are.

My whole life
has been one long
improvisation.
I've considered going to Hell
& calling aloud
upon the spirits of the dead,
who promise
Heaven, Paradise,
higher reincarnations
—together or apart.
Quite often

the world is not round.

I used to
imagine
my own funeral.
There were
stars & a half moon
in the sky,
a dark hole
in the ground,
& a wooden casket
lowered
into the shadows.
There were
fragrances & voices,
shapes
without faces.
Gravediggers,
with unshaven skin,
with rolled-up sleeves
& shovels,
smoked cigarettes
& tossed dirt,
hid
everything
that didn't matter.
They smelled
of tobacco
& of pine forest.
The air had
an electric stink.

Who knows
what lies
underground,
beneath
the hard, black
earth that the summer
heat exposes?

I told myself
that if I died
before you,
I'd come back
to the apartment
we shared.
This would be me:
a light on in the kitchen
when you return late
from a business trip
between Christmas
& New Year's Eve,
footsteps outside
your bedroom,
the dog
moving its head
in obedient circles,
as I dance in the space
above the kitchen table,
a corkscrew
pushed off
one of the shelves,
the television screen
a crisscross

of black, wavy strips
as you watch
a Netflix movie.
Your cheeks
would sag
like wet
laundry, your shoulders
sink down
into a slouch.
I'd attach
myself to the very couch
where the one
who would come after me
left her satin bras.
You'd watch paranormal
shows on television,
call out
into the dark
rooms of the apartment,
fill tables
with recording equipment,
& hold séances
with Ouija boards.
Do you want
to speak to me?
Why are you
in our home?
& everything
would grow heavy,
like the air
is wearing weights.

She would want
to help you stop
the haunting,
her body a live wire
throwing off a current.
This would bring
you closer together;
you would
pour Merlot
& clink glasses.
I would not
show myself.
An empty
nothing
searching
for something
that was
never there.

José Armando

Don't say
these things.

Paloma

I don't want
to justify
how I feel
—my diffuse existence,
my trap
of contradictions.

Sometimes,
tangled
in the sheets, I dream
about water gushing
through the window.
The water opens,
swallows me,
& I'm drowning,
dropping, dropping,
the force of the water
dissolves my flesh
& leaves my bones
polished, white
—until I mirror the sky
& have no memory,
& no future.

& whether there is a god
or no god,
it doesn't matter.
God is outside
the equation.
Despite the many times

I pray
not to wake up,
I do.
& the muffled silence
doesn't belong
to any real world.

If I am to be brave,
I want to learn
to swim
in these waters,
in their irresistible
chiaroscuro,
in the weight
of their insistent
turbulence.

I can't love
anything
or anyone
—until
I've dug deeper
& deeper into my broken
self & pulled
beauty & poetry
from the shards.
I don't want
your arms around me
—until
I'm no longer
jagged.

Right now, I can only
tear you
to ribbons.

My chemistry
is confusion.
I've sat
in the chairs of dozens
of specialists,
who study methods
to make my brain bloom
like a sunflower.
I've swallowed
a spectrum of pills
formulated to untangle me,
& it's all just
a Band-Aid
covering a wound
so deep,
it's gone septic.

That invasion
you feel
in your capillaries
is an infection.
It will kill you
if you let it.

José Armando

I want to help you.
When you are raging,
ready to throw
a sea of pots & pans at me,
when you're ready to beat
your chest, I want
to hold you tighter,
in this world
of time & consequence.
I want to kiss you,
so you remember
what you are, because
when you remember,
you want nothing
more than for me
to hold you
& kiss you,
kiss you good.
Even if you say
this is not true,
not at all,
it is still true.
You are assailed
by longing
for exactly
what we have.

Paloma

He wants
to save me,
but even
his voice is too much
for me
right now.
& who
would he be saving?
I'm not this woman
whose name
he cries out for,
no little turtle dove,
Paloma, that he can rescue,
toting its small
breast, downy head,
broken wing, cradling
it in the hollow
of his palm.
I am more
demon
than goddess,
more war
than peace.
Only I can
wrap my arms
around my own darkness
& make it
a rainbow.

José Armando

I'll help you
see beauty in things
you never
noticed before
that are all around you.
Look:
a tender
sickle of grass bending
under the weight
of a bead of dew
with the moon
in its eye / a suggestion
of moonlight,
the Hialeah sky tiled
with rows
of rippling white.

Paloma

You want me
to lie down
in fragrant leaves & see
poetry in the smell
of sweet decay,
sparks under the earth:
worms aerating
soil, seeds breaking
from shells.
None of that is real.
Not yet.
My world is made of harsh,
solid words: Zoloft
& Prozac, Sarafem
& Lexapro, Luvox
& Oleptro, dysfunction
& imbalance,
serotonin,
norepinephrine,
& dopamine.
I am trapped
in chemicals,
hormones, science.

I've been fighting so hard
& for so long,
I have nothing left.
No compass, no north.
Let me find my own
way back to you.

Shadow

Her life hurts
like a dream
in which no one finds
the missing
baby. She is that mother, desperate
for a newborn
she never bore.
She's never
given birth to anything
but emptiness.

Give birth to yourself, then.
It takes some pushing,
but you'll emerge.

Paloma

Until I unfold into myself,
something will always warn
me, that in whatever direction
I head, I will wind up
full fathom five.
& I'm already
being pulled down
towards the bottom.

Tethered
between land & horizon,
I'm already
floating nowhere:
I need one fewer thing
mooring me.
You anchor me
to nothing.
Please let me
be loosened.

José Armando

You slipped
into my teenage summer
ten years ago,
& hovered
like a black-eyed storm,
calming my center.
It's only the outer
bands of your system
that are destructive.
If you leave now,
I'll be a desolated
plain. I'll be the morning
after a hurricane.
If you break
my heart, I will age
twenty years in seconds.
I want to be
with you.
If you're half an orange,
I'm half an orange
—not necessarily the better
half, but the other.
& apart,
there is nothing
to hold
the juice under our skin,
We'd become
desiccated,
dry things.
Husks of ourselves.

Shadow

The morning after
a hurricane
is not the worst place
to be.
It is the point
at which rebuilding begins.

Paloma

I'm tired
of being defined by words
like thyroid,
cortisol,
& brain chemistry.
The real world
enters me:
& I stay up
late & drink
Cuba libres.

I gorge
on my own heart.
If you don't
let me go,
I'll devour yours
next.

The rum doesn't hit
my throat like a fist,
but crawls
in smooth, teasing
fingers, bringing me back
to old days,
to a space outside
of space. Last night,
you told me
you loved me
& I said, thanks,
not because

I don't love you,
but because
I'm a rat in a maze
I keep forgetting
I built by myself.

When life unravels,
it does in ways I never expected.

During these hours
of perplexity
& private sorrow
in Hialeah,
I am empty,
I am glass.
I stare
at the quarter moon hanging
above the trees, their
branches pregnant
with unripe mangoes.

Everything
is transitory,
vaguely out of time.
I'm engulfed
in the incessant
drone of things
happening.
I want
to be lit afire:
orange shapes
that'll flicker & deepen

in color, ashes billowing
with fury.

I imagine
blowing on a flame, harder
& harder, until it becomes
a conflagration
that swallows the world.
But nothing ignites.
There is no spark
to start the world burning.

The only thing constant
is the incessant voice
in my bones,
screaming doom & decay.
We are dying,
alone, together,
all the same.

Sometimes, I think
I am missing
the key to unlock
my mind
from all this gloom
that rings in my spine
like a doomsday chime.

I'd like to toss off
this cloak of heavy
& wear a delicate
robe of glee,

& sometimes,
I think it might
just be that easy
to do, just change
out my mood
like a shirt
I've forgotten
to launder.

Shadow

You will change when you're ready.

José Armando

You are who you are:
the girl I love:
the girl
who will break
my heart: who's broken
my heart already,
& will do it again.
There will be
darkness,
but there will also be
daylight.
In my arms,
you'll hold yourself
together
against whatever it is
that tears you apart—
the pull
of your own limbs,
your heart,
the greater pull of the world.

Paloma

I am who I am.

Shadow

You are much more than that.

José Armando

& you are enough.

Paloma

I am a chemical wasteland,
but something
is whispering "I am complete"
beneath it all.
& I need to find out
what "complete"
really means.
I can't
make any promises
that I will wake
next to you
tomorrow
& want
to be anywhere,
& it's not that your arms
aren't the only ones
I want wrapped
around my body.
It's just that I need
the space
for sanity
to seep in & buffer
me like a blanket.
I need that blanket
around me
more
than I need
any arms right now.
I am no princess
you can rescue.

& rescuing damsels
is heavy labor.
Let me rescue myself,
& if I can tear down
the tower
I've walled myself in,
maybe I'll find my way
back to you.
But I need
to find my way back
to myself first.

Shadow

The northbound train
is approaching the station.
Step back
from the platform edge.
Please wait
until passengers
exit the train
before boarding.

José Armando

I wanted to be the one
to loosen
the knot
between your brows
& find a soft
place within you.

In my dreams,
I can not only see
your lines & bones
but taste them,
smell them, feel
them on my skin,
& hear the shape
of your lips
ring all around me
like shaken bells.

The sky might lose
its way
& the stars rip.
If you let me,
I'd follow you over
rivers of stones.

I don't want to catch that train
without you.

Paloma

It isn't my train.

For the first time
I can remember,
I am feeling more certain
that everything happens
as it is meant to,
that it will be okay.
That I deserve
to find happy
—whatever that is.

I don't think
it's something
you find in someone else.

I think it might be
a wise voice
in the pit
of our bellies that tells us
to carry on
when the days weep
like ripe black sapote,
& threaten to fall.

I will write a manifesto
for when the sky
is the color of chaos.

José Armando

It is not a story with a good ending.
Something
in my chest
will tear apart
—something
grown over,
tangled,
uncared for.

I don't have a choice
but to let you untangle
yourself, but remember,
I am also a fierce,
frayed knot
you are ripping
out at the root.

Silence swallows
the apartment we share
& I'm suspended
in the dark
warmth of its throat.

Paloma

I'm not looking at that train
as something
I want to jump
in front of,
but something
I want to carry me.
But right now,
it's not my train.
You go,
catch it alone
for now.

We are not
two halves of the same
orange. We are each of us
an orange, complete
on its own.
If we cut ourselves
in half
& press
the pulp against
the other half,
we'd just rot.

Shadow

This manifesto:
Shall we do this?
Are you ready?

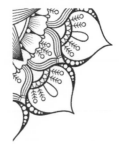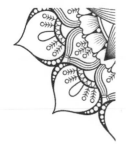

Interlude

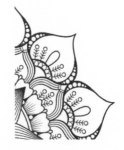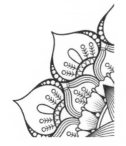

Shadow

When her legs first stretched
themselves to stand
with strength
she did not yet know
she possessed,
I was the voice
by her bassinet,
that gave her reason
to giggle at dust motes
suspended in sunbeams.
She almost
lost
the eye
for small miracles,
& my voice, for a while,
was a dog whistle
to her ears, just out
of frequency.
But I kept speaking.
Until, one day, she heard me.
I have been waiting,
calling,
sitting beside her
through the long spaces
in-between
desire & contentment,
so elusive,
but waiting,
through the summa
cum laude

master's degree
from the university,
through the job interviews,
the commutes
to a job she should love,
but doesn't,
through nights
of twisted sheets.

Now
she is ready
for
militance,
for strength,
or at least solace;
maybe a manifesto
whose words
will tingle
her bones
& turn her
into something
greater
than herself.
She's eager
to create
a new world,
to unravel
the knots
that were tied
long ago.

She is ready

now,
to remember
how to laugh
at the littlest things.
Because
when there is hope,
excitement rises
from the back
of her neck,
an exquisite
pulse turns on
the nerve endings
in every millimeter
of flesh.

She is human—mutable.
Nothing
in the world
is ever otherwise.

*

It's 75 degrees
at the Metrorail station
in Hialeah.

Paloma,
by the time
you head back
to your childhood
home,
it will be hot

again—because
Hialeah is very
temperamental.

A bit like you.

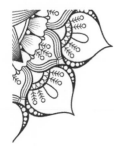
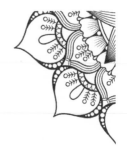

Part II

Happy, Okay?

Two years later

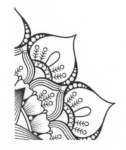
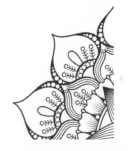

The Happy, Okay? Manifesto
Found Poems for When the Sky Is the Color of Chaos
(Draft 51)

Article I: I Will Remember the Motion of the Moon

Article II: I Will Shed the Parts of Myself that Don't
Really Matter

Article III I Will Acknowledge My Pain is Real

Article IV: I Will Reparent Myself

Article V: I Will Walk Away

Article VI: I Will Not Carry a Country

Article VII: I Will Not Expect Others to Understand

Article VIII: I Will Dance to the Music

Article IX: I Will Dance to the Music (Again)

Article X: I Will Dance to the Music (Again & Again)

Article XI: I Will Dance to the Music (Always)

Article XII: I Will Embrace Loneliness

Article XIII: I Will Believe in Friendship

Article XIV: I Will Let Myself Be Loved

Article XV: I Will Stay Away from Married Men

Article XVI: I Will Practice Self-Talk

Article XVII: I Will Save Myself with Stories

Article XVIII: I Will Remember to Breathe

Article XIX: I Will Practice Gratitude

Article XX: I Will Practice Self-Care

Article XXI: I Will Remember to Self-Soothe

Article XXII: I Will Acknowledge That I Don't Know
Which Way the Road Goes

Article XXIII: I Will Embrace Miami

Article XXIV: I Will Allow Myself to Splurge

Article XXV: I Will Ask for Help

Article XXVI: I Will Keep the Faith

Article I

I Will Remember the Motion of the Moon

I don't always know who I am,
but I know I'm not the kind of girl
who can be contained
in thick black eyeliner
& lace underwear.
I'm not audacious enough
to know what I want
& what I am made of.
The anxiety
of being looked at,
of being looked into,
can make me fold into myself.
I am still learning I am too many
things to explore all at once,
& unfolding
is a petal-by-petal process.

I remember the young girl I used to be,
sitting on my father's lap,
his chin resting on top of my head,
his newspaper folded
the same way every day,
a girl with inexhaustible longing
for more—more of what?—
who was told who to be
& when to behave.
The girl I am today
is still eager for fire,
& still terrified to burn.

I once played a game of
"let's pretend to be
anything but me"
& wrapped my leg over the back
of a motorcycle, hoisted myself
onto the cracked vinyl seat,
& the hot air ran its fingers
through my hair &
fumbled my budding breasts shaped
like unopened lotus blooms.
Guilt, euphoria,
& dim apprehension
stirred in this temporary wild girl,
as I tried to imagine
the woman I would become
in twenty & some years.
Would I become someone soft
whose arms are an oasis
or would my tongue cut & terrify?

I've learned since,
that I'm sometimes
wicked, broken, & lost—
& sometimes
I live my life with a chattering passion,
& also with devotion & charity.
I'm a jigsaw puzzle
still waiting to be solved.

I've come to accept
the dry, parched desert
inside of me.
If they cut me open
they'd find the Sahara.
Sometimes, the world
gets so big so fast
that I can shrink
& fall through the cracks
like an ant.
When the night is furrowed,
the clouds are bruised
plums, I've come to accept
that I will turn in circles,
until I no longer
know where it is in this world
I can hide.
I dream that I can no longer feel
my own flesh, my hard-jutting bones,
the soft places, folds & crevices.
I become plenty of nothing.

My changes are like
the motion of the moon:
one night, a crescent cupped gently
like an open hand, the next, a round
cast iron skillet that might break you.
I will remember
that the moon
has her cycles,
& so do I:
continuous in my
waxing and waning.

Outside the window, a breeze comes up,
a phantom thing
from out of nowhere,
& blows seeds
from an acacia tree. I hear a motorcycle,
& I see a wild, wild, girl hoisted
onto the cracked vinyl seat,
the hot air running its fingers
through her hair. & I want to tell her
that I still don't know what I want
& what I am made of.
Sometimes, I am an oasis.
Sometimes, my tongue cuts & terrifies.

But I'm okay—even when I'm
wicked, broken, & lost, I
live my life with a chattering passion,
& also with devotion & charity.

Article II

I Will Shed the Parts of Myself That Don't Really Matter

I wanted to be the kind
of girl who'd steal smokes
from her mother's purse
& booze
from her father's cabinet,
who'd sneak into R-rated
movies at the local theater & lose
her virginity
to an older boy
who had his own car
& liked to do it
in the backseat, become
a dangerous girl
who'd drive
in the middle of the road
& wouldn't obey
stop signs.

I imagined that girl,
hurried, naked
—sweating
with a forbidden
lover on her twin-sized bed,
under striped
sheets & posters of boy bands,
feeling no regret
when daylight came, turning
the sky from purple
to blue, & then to a shocking
bright light.

I wanted to be wild.
But I barely understood
the language of flirting,
dating, love, passion.
When my papa broke
the porcelain vases, & my mama
went to bed with a crust of tears
drying on her cheeks,
I stared at the dark
television, & in the curve
of the screen, my reflection
was at the end
of a long,
black hallway.

I walked outside
& the world looked flat
& the sky was the color
of the sidewalk
& the people on the street
looked like people on any
street. The clouds above me
were bland.
Everything was bland.

That was before
I learned to sharpen
my heart like a bayonet.
I know that even if I pull it out,
I will not bleed to death.
I can always piece myself together,
& give myself back to me.

I can shed the parts of myself
that don't really matter.

Article III

I Will Acknowledge My Pain Is Real

I once met a girl in rehab. Her name was Sarah. She told
horror stories from her childhood. I can't stop
imagining her, a child asleep on soft pillows
with puffy clouds. Blue & purple butterflies
with glittery wings. Blue & purple painted fairies.
Blue & purple unicorns with rainbow horns.
The smell of gin & tobacco crawling
between her sheets. Her father's eyes dry & red.
She tries to close her thighs. His hands wrap
around her throat, thumbs pressing,
her head a champagne cork he wants to pop off.
She is numb, a blue & purple butterfly.
It's easy to understand
how something so delicate can learn
to fly crooked with bruised wings.
But in my case, there's no why.
It's all about how: neurochemicals & imbalance,
Nothing makes me or breaks me.
I'm just built this way.
My pain is as real as anyone else's.

Article IV

I Will Reparent Myself

I'll write about the papa I always wanted:
He sits on a balcony, serious & dignified,
wearing sandals with interlocking straps
of light & dark leather. He leans on
the balustrade, watches the street,
& the man who walks with a limp,
& the buses that push & pull
at their brakes & turn street corners,
watches the lines of laundry, strung
between gray walls, stained by azaleas,
watches me ride the neighbor's bicycle.
As he worries about darting cars
& bumps in the sidewalk, the late
evening sun settles upon his face,
dust particles
float in the sweltering air.

I'll long for him, my noisy, careless father,
his heavy step, his deep voice filling up
the rooms, his laugh a steady vibration
against the drums inside my ears. His face
was less angled when he laughed
—soft as sunrise—& his jaw
less strong, less square.

I'll write about a papa who helped me
with complicated homework,
when the numbers in the math book
wouldn't hold still—numbers like swarming
gnats that buzz about my head.
As I completed the assignments, the world
had an ethereal stillness, a colorful tranquility.

With a knife, my papa broke a melon,
revealing its pink center, its myriad of seeds.
He reached for a pink slice, brought it
to his mouth, & sank his teeth into it.
Pink juice ran out, gathered & quivered
on his chin. Or he peeled an orange, lost
himself in the color & segments & sparkle
of the pulp. He offered me a piece of fruit
—feeding is a kind of love.

If you do it right,
it won't be clear who's filling whom.

When my face drains of color,
& there's something starved about it
—like some small, feral animal, something
hunted—I'll write about father-daughter
car rides around Port-au-Prince, windows
down, dashboard peeling in sunlight,
seatbelts frayed like catfish whiskers.
Sometimes we remain quiet, listening to
the thread of the tires run along
the asphalt, how they collect pebbles
& drop them back. He'll clasp
my hand, Papa; squeeze it, feeling
the warmth inside, the pulsing heat of blood.

In these stories, he'll sometimes take me
to the mountains, turn up the music in the car,
until it is a giant bass roar & I can't hear
anything else, not even my own mind. The sky
is blue, the mountains are green, & sheep
graze in the fields. The cherries are dark
& shine on the treetops. We climb higher
& higher, the road twisting & turning
& cars flying by in a manner both dangerous
& natural. On our way back,
the engine growls as the sun recedes, shady patches
deepen with shadows. I am happy
for this moment—my father breathing the same air
I breathe, our hearts beating to the same rhythm.

When I am lost in time, unhinged,
when parts of me trail off, disconnected,
I'll become him,
for myself,
this tender father
—without the kind of loneliness
that settles in my chest, a small, hard knot
—without the kind of sorrow
that tries to take me out of myself.
I'll become him in those epic days of quarter
life, finding himself, verging on success,
on failure, his own father inside him.
& I'll become him, this father
whose mouth is not dirty with rage,
but rather honeyed with affection.
Both father & daughter, I'll tuck myself
in the warmth of my own bed,
where I'll read the Brothers Grimm,
& verses from King James Bible.

I'll whisper, I love you—to myself, on his behalf.
I'll whisper, I love you—to my noisy, careless father,
his heavy step, his deep voice filling up
the rooms, his laugh a steady vibration
against the drums inside my ears. His face
is less angled when he laughs—soft as sunrise
—& his jaw less strong, less square.

Article V

I Will Walk Away

1.

I'll remember that people
are not always safe places.
They're people, like me.
Sometimes they are traps
that turn time
solid,
that burn my tongue
& lodge in my throat.
People can both hold you
& push you away,
suffocate with tension & confusion.

Allegiance waxes
& flows like tides
you can neither predict nor chart.
Sisters swear they'll keep secrets they later blurt out.
Mothers don't choose their words with much care:
they slap you with them, unable
to understand your longing
to be something other
than what you are, to be somewhere
other than here, that everything
feels transitory, out of time.
Fathers fall into moods
so dark & long & private
that they lose their train of thought
& sit blinking,
walled in thick dissatisfaction.

Theatrics steal your sleep,
until it all feels like a nightmare,
& you believe
dawn will transform everything.
The Egyptians said the sun burnt up
each evening & rekindled in the morning
—a fresh torch for the day.
You stay up all night to prove it,
star-gazing, star-thinking,
star-dreaming. Under all those stars,
you realize the truth
you can barely face
when it is daylight:
You need to break free.

When you are loved, you are less spectral,
less insubstantial, less invisible.
Your body is a tangible thing,
shoulders & arms & hands.
But in unhealthy love: people
engulf you in a drone of
voices buzzing with bad ideas,
until there's nothing
but chaos in your veins.

Walk away.

Whether you stay or not,
you can love them.
Whether you stay or not,
—people are born, people die,
people eat, drink, sing in the shower,
clip their nails, wipe their asses,
do the everyday things people do
as they live. Petunias nod yes, yes
to the wind. Brown-winged butterflies
mingle, & bees scribble
over the pistils of hibiscus flowers.
The sun shoots black spots
into your eyes when you forget to blink,
while the wind moans
like a low fire.

2.

Jose Armando, I was of the water,
current and undertow,
murky and turbulent:
a channel, an eddy, old, old,
like the universe,
rhythm low and telling,
waves breaking,
sucking in,
rumbling out.

Rooms flooded
and flowed with my tide,
walls stretched and buckled,
and you, my Captain,
you felt the upsurge of it all
as you cleaved my currents.

Do you know that Hope
can be as sharp
as a piranha's teeth?

José Armando, I was in the water:
legs and shoulders burning
through the waves.
I sloshed with the current,
the world in my throat,
rose up like a lungfish,
flayed by sea and wind.

I hoped to emerge,
reborn,
shimmering.

Article VI

I Will Not Carry a Country

1.

Papa says, where we come from,
no one has the luxury of self-loathing
—they are too busy rising from rubble
& building castles with what lies in the streets.

He looks at me like I am an orphan
Mama found swaddled in rags on the doorstep
one morning. He asks how this miserable
creature with so much to live for
could choose to wash her cheeks with tears,
& clear her throat with screams.

Mama says, "Girl,
you are like a rubber band.
You can stretch as far as you'd like to."
I've come to learn
that, stretched too far,
a rubber band will snap.

I've come to learn
that when I rupture,
I become shrapnel,
marring the faces of those around me
with wounded disgust.

2.

I dream of a place
where no one knows my name,
where I am not beckoned like a pet
who knows a trick
to make their master's mouth curl into a grin,
where no one expects
a clever remark or even a smile
—where people are more indifferent
toward me than towards
a loose stone in their path.
How kind it would be to be kicked to the curb,
& left to lie in the dust,
where no one can try to reassemble me
into something I have no interest in becoming,
where I can be free
of the burdensome load
of carrying a country,
culture,
and history
on my back.
I will carry my fair share,
but I can't carry it all.
And I am free to create
my own place with my own rules,
separate from what
has been handed down to me.

Article VII

I Will Not Expect Others to Understand

1.

In my family albums, some of the pictures of my papa
are blurred, in soft light, otherwise indistinct. Others
are sharp, the eyebrows dark, thin, & arching.
His lips are full, like pomegranates, his chin firm.
In one photo, his eyes are dangerous. He is hard angles,
his body could cut you, if you didn't know
the way to move around him.

Sometimes, a man, a father, will look at you in
ways that make you want to die.
Sometimes, in ways that make your heart
open like a moonflower. You'll see how afraid he is
that you might fracture into the dots
of a pointillist painting. You'll see how he is certain
he is to blame. You'll see desperation
you missed in his eyes before.

My papa once bought me a bouquet
of red & pink azaleas from a farmers' market
in the mountains of Port-au-Prince, & the flowers
filled the air with their musky smell; the chapel's bells
rang four o'clock, & the cowbells on
mini-ice cream trucks clanged down the dusty road.
The azaleas curled before I remembered to vase them,
& I cried for so long that my papa replaced them
with begonias & snapdragons,
small but already blooming,
their fuzzy pink tongues
sticking out like a taunt.
They didn't thrive either,
but before they died,
I brought them to my face
to inhale their sweetness.

People don't always understand
when I tell them:
where there's roughness,
there's often tenderness too.
My muscles ache with pangs
of longing for a father I know
existed alongside the one
who moved through stark murkiness,
overwhelming sadness,
the one who lost God & clan
because they couldn't share his secret grief.
The one whose fists became bludgeons
when he didn't know what else to do.

It's physical, a deep longing,
as much for that other father
as for the second me,
who also resides alongside the first me in photos,
a second girl trying to push out from my torso,
to struggle free from my bones.

My papa sits in his rocking
chair, & I'm in the background of the photo,
holding the azaleas that must have been nodding
in the first evening breezes.
I'm oddly positioned within the space,
my arm cut off by the frame of the camera.
& all I want right now is for my papa
to gather me up in the circle of his arms
& carry me to comfort.
I remember that my throat hurt that night,
dry in a place my tongue couldn't reach, an ache
outside myself, on the soft of my palate.
If you stare at a photograph long enough,

it flutters,
& the eyes inside nearly wink.

2.

I let booze warm my cheeks
as I listen to the quiet in the room
& imagine myself as someone else.
Someone I could admire.
I have friends I know as intimately as
the moles on my skin, & they don't see
the me behind the forced smiles.
I spend hours with them, laughing woodenly
at their silly jokes,
the crushes of boys they'll forget,
the same way I want to forget
those hours filled with
the secret
of what I am inside this skin.

The few times I let myself slip out,
like a python crawling out of the brush,
they look at me & laugh & say,
"Girl, you got everything going for you:
Handsome novio, top of our class,
scholarship to university in Miami,
parents who love you. Damn, we adore you.
We all want to be you."

&, "Get a grip."

As if I can grip the tsunami
stealing my breath.
Then I sleep
away the gushes of pain in my lungs.

I dream that I strangle another curly-haired
woman, who turns out to be myself.

3.

Look at all these people around us.
Each with a set destination, a place
where people are waiting for their arrival:
families, jobs, brunch dates, appointments.
Where am I going?
To college classrooms, to sit for hours,
& listen to a professor drone on
& on & on, on subjects
that should delight me.
For a degree that will bring me a career,
more money.
Enough money to buy a house,
a life, filled with things
that should make me happy.
But then, it's just a lifetime
of coming & going,
coming & going,
to work, to home,
to one obligation after another.
All futile motions,
all a march towards the end.
I don't have to match
their stride
or follow the direction
they are headed.
My feet forge their own trail.

I'm happy, okay?

Article VIII

I Will Dance to the Music

A boy named Vincent taught me
how to slow dance,
low dance, & fast dance.
We belted out Salt-N-Pepa,
crooned to Coolio, & swooned to the New Kids
on The Block.
We played our music loud,
so the bass thumped in our sternums.
We were too young for the dance club,
but we imagined
dirty neon lights dangling from ceiling beams
that flickered on & off without rhythm.
I could hear the music
in my chest, vibrating, waiting,
a wave that would flatten my thoughts, wash
them away with a mindless, insistent staccato.
I wanted to be the pulse of this music
—as it pulled me out of myself, unhooked pelvises,
butts pivoting on their axes. Cocktail
stirrers littering the dance floor.
Every evil thought in my head
dropped in the rhythm.

When anxiety creeps from the base of my skull,
& makes my scalp tingle & tighten, when it swells
beneath my breastbone, I turn on the radio, close

my eyes & walk into the music, into shadows
of imagined night clubs, & sticky nights
press against my skin, until perspiration beads
my upper lip. In the musical based on my life,
the voice of the lead singer is strong
& unlabored even when stretching for notes
in upper registers. I hang on every phrase,
awaiting the next pause, streak or curve.
There is a rhythm in my movements.

I am a pulse.

Article IX

I Will Dance to the Music (Again)

In the plume of heat that engulfs
the afternoon air, Hialeah
parades down Calle Ocho.
The city is a livewire, flicking like a dare.
Pockets of worry have been torn
from sweat-soaked shirts,
& I've found something
inside myself,
asleep for so very long
I don't know the word for it.
But there must be a word for it.

You forget your troubles,
like a single clove
hidden
among the soggy chunks
of eggplant & okra
in the legumes
they sell at the food stand.

The beat of the band
becomes hands on your hips,
& you forget about gravity.
You fall into me,
your soles slipping
on jagged terrain.

As you dance, you lean back
into my chest
& I don't know your name yet,
but allow the back of your head
to nestle in my sternum.

You find something inside yourself,
asleep for so very long
you don't know the word for it.
But there must be a word for it.

There's a word
for most things in the world
But we both know
some things are indefinable,
untranslatable,
unspeakable.
The word is lost,
forgotten,
almost remembered,
almost found.
Sanctified.

In the plume of heat that engulfs
the afternoon air,
you are a livewire
flicking like a dare.

M.J. Fievre

Article X

I Will Dance to the Music (Again & Again)

Port-au-Prince erupts in an ecstatic
fête of pulsating music & swirling
dancers. Carnival: Thousands of frantic
souls in the Champ-de-Mars—marching, bouncing.

> Blur of colors—purple for justice, green
> for faith & gold for power. Beads. Feathers.
> Sequins. Glitter. Majestic kings & queens.
> The introverted become merry makers.

Jenny & I shake rainbow maracas,
both frightened & elated. We hardly
breathe, swallowed by this bacchanalian mass,
this colorful crush of humanity.

> We throng among the glamorous & keen,
> the bizarre, the hungry, the in-between.

The bizarre, the hungry, the in-between
dance to rara rhythms & spicy sounds.
Revelers as we've never before seen
trail the bann a pye on the heated ground.

We drink Prestige beer & smoke unfiltered
    cigarettes. Forget heartache & raw pain.

We follow the hordes of dancers, slathered
    in body paint, oil & mud—we're insane.

Nèg Gwo Siwo lead the parade, bodies
coated with tallow, cane syrup & sweat,
entranced in the pure rasin melodies,
the deep rhythm of trombones & trumpets.

    We lose ourselves in the Carnival.
    In the delirious crowd, ça n' va pas mal.

Article XI

I Will Dance to the Music (Always)

The music man sits in his wicker chair. Hands trace
intricate patterns, directing an orchestra.
Music sheets nap on top of a piano
in the corner of his studio. He sees
his wife knitting on the red
padded sofa, feels her silent anticipation.

He French kisses his shiny saxophone
blows a tentative do, ré, mi.
The notes tremble, then with deep
clarity, reach out
& wrap themselves around him.

Eyes downcast,
he commands the music like a snake
charmer working a deep trance.
Cheeks puff & fingers glide quickly
along the clean, oiled valves.

He turns into a merman;
shares with the darkness
the elusive beauty of true, clear notes
that ring off the ceiling, that sweat
the moisture of the cool April night.

The melody lifts out the window, past
the coconut & palm trees,
down the ravine,
to the dark paved road;
the sax coaxes the weeds,
& calls to Baron Samedi
in the cemetery beyond,
burnished & brooding,
ripples the still
surface of the mosquito-dotted lake
on the edge of the city,
green water merging with the night.

His music is the heartbeat of a last kiss.
His eyes see his beloved
on that sofa, trace the curves
of her flowered dress
& robust shoulders,
as her lips smooth
into the shapes of love.

His lips barely touch the mouthpiece,
his tongue teases
the metal into looping percussion,
into a waterfall of clearing rainbows
pouring into the soul,
an evening adieu.

Article XII

I Will Embrace Loneliness

When I was a child,
Mother entered my room
for bedtime prayers.
Jésus, Marie, Joseph, je vous donne mon coeur,
mon âme, mon esprit et ma vie.
Mother's arms were slightly raised,
fingers unfurled, like she was trying not to fall.
She looked placid
on the edge of sleep.
On the wall, Jesus followed her gestures
with his dark eyes,
ready to weep real tears.

I let my fingers feel the rosary beads
Papa had given me for my first communion
shift across my palms, a calibrated slither
against my skin as I prayed.
I listened to the crickets,
the first of the evening birds,
the breeze rustling the grapevines.
I felt an aching sense of loss.

I ended prayers the way
I ended conversations: abruptly,
without lengthy prelude or false closure.
Amen,

& I was gone.

I've learned to embrace
the loneliness of being Catholic.
In my small church,
dark & cool, the soft, blue tinge
& irregular shapes of stained glass
tiles depict the stories of saints & scenes
from the Bible where the heroes carried,
the weight of their destinies.
I love the chanting
of Veni Creator Spiritu,
the statue of the Virgin Mary with her smooth,
serene face & her outstretched arms
—her courage in loneliness.

Father Martin wears an elaborate robe
of gold & silver threads
that sparkle in candlelight.
Incense weaves into the weft of his clothes.
When he gazes into a mirror
& into his own eyes, does he fear
the proximity of that other face
glaring wildly at him through the glass?
What dreams does he keep sheathed,
sharp & deep in his heart?

On Sundays, head bowed & hands
together in front of my face,
I make my way toward the altar;
I genuflect, kneels, tilt my head back
& stick out my tongue

to receive the Body of Christ.
I am awed by centuries of ritual—& loneliness.
It rushes me with something dark & heady.
& I embrace it, because I am
not alone in my solitude.

Article XIII

I'll Believe in Friendship

1.

I dream
of a trapdoor
into a room that spins.

Distances:
words inch their way
into my head,
itching like bad ideas:
meters & acres
& points of no return.

How many feet
to the pavement?
How many hurts,
how many
broken bones?

2.

New Harmony, Indiana.
The serene boondocks.
A girl named Katie.

A tandem bike.
A minute bottle

of vodka jungle juice
smuggled
into the Barn Abbey.

Tornado sirens,
Midwestern snacks,
midnight escapes,
& the obscure ploy
to trespass
& skinny dip
in a pool.

Let's do it!
(Her words or mine?)

A man lounged
on a mattress
behind a pickup truck
en route for Illinois,
& Katie & I
told each other a story
about a broken heart.

3.

On the balustrade
I wonder
if I'll see
the tops of everything.
& whether I'll look back
to see my old self
still

on the pavement.

My doppelganger:
a passing glimpse,
the recognition
coming
a few seconds later.

How many shadows
to become whole?
How many
cracked shadows
& shadowed cracks?

4.

We tripped
over broken pavements,
singing
to the moon.

I remember
the laughter
—not hers,
mine,
but born from hers—
laughter
that ran down my cheeks
in twittering tears.

We made up stories,
wanting our writing

to move
the day forward.
We added words,
made up words,
used other worlds' words,
& watched newborn worlds
as they emerged.

5.

If my fragments reconcile,
what happens
when the whole
pulses
with severed screams?

I am neither
asleep nor awake,
but in some other realm,
purgatory.

Such a tulip-soft day.
A bird makes its call,
two quick dips
& then
mangled laughter.

Memories go to noise,
satirical
& uncontrollable.

6.

Secrets were whispered,
confessions brought forth,
as we blended
with shadows,
in a quest
to discover
the cathedral labyrinth
in dark
Indiana hours.

7.

Of course,
I can pretend
shadows are solid
& slick.

Who'll go to the river
& return my ashes?

I let the night
slow down around me.
I let
the night slow down
around me.

8.

& just like that—

the sun came out
in Indiana.
Turned out
I'd been staring straight
into its face
for several lifetimes.

& peace settled again—again.
& peace settled again
again.
& peace settled
again.

Again.

Article XIV

I Will Let Myself Be Loved

1.

In photos with my sister, I am always bigger:
heavier, thicker boned, thoughtless in the way
I claim space. She is skinny, but fills the air
beyond the boundaries of her delicate frame.
My sister is water to my fire.
She's the yin to my shambolic yang,
when inordinate rage & breath-catching irritation
build within me,
when my fury comes like one hundred horns
& one hundred bells,
my nerves a chorus
of plucked strings,
a quiver of quivering. When the blood
in my fingertips pulse,
& my jaws cramp from clenching
tight to keep my screams
quiet from the night,
she is safety, warmth,
& temperance in a dangerous world,
a world in which I can never trust
myself, because even a day that seems mundane
holds in its purposeful
or dreamy breaths
the possibility of precipitous rage, the heaves
from my body terribly loud: frightening.

My sister hugs me & I let her, & I hold on,
her heartbeat against my chest. Its beautiful,
crazy boom boom. A drum beating.
A cup of sparking fireflies.
As I cry, her fingers nestle
in the ridges of my spine.
Not all arms are an oasis,
but some arms
can span the vast contradictions
of who I am,
& they hold me safe.

2.

At the farmers' market on Calle Ocho,
our stomachs gurgle like lava lamps,
so we buy cherries & spit the pits at each other.
The shells, glistening with saliva & clinging fruits,
freckle the Miami asphalt.
We lick juice from the webs between our fingers,
take in the sweet scent.
How miraculous this world.
We see it all the way we want to be seen.

3.

I was of the water,
you were of the air,
and we both hungered
      for a place we didn't remember.
There was a craving
      in your joints, José Armando,
as I opened up in waves
      and left you dizzy
      and surrounded
        by the deafening roar
          of the blood in your veins.
—as   I walked away.

I've returned
to your shores,
years later,
this time for good.
And I've found you:
    waiting,
        ready,
even though
you remember
the fury
of my summer storms.

I play the banjo
on your naked thighs,
your magnificent calves,
your dimpled knees,
every particle
alive in the filtered
sunshine
under
the mango trees—
branch tips
thick with fruit.

The sun pulls
the sky
into its heat,
scorches it
bare of clouds.
I am
reborn,
shimmering.

Article XV

I Will Stay Away from Married Men

1.

There is no pulse, no rhythm beating
through the layers of my skin, through
my blood-filled veins. Once
I was a woman. But I gave myself over
& over until I no longer
noticed the oranges & reds of Hialeah's
fire bushes.

The night we met, you & I traded stories,
our voices growing softer as my shoulders
pressed against yours. You traced
my eyebrows & deepened my frown
lines with your shaky fingers.
"Are you cold?" I asked. "Nerves,"
you answered, rushed, breathless,
your words so sweet in their sonic grace.

2.

Above the shotgun houses,
the clouds are storm purple
& the sky is swollen.
An unkindness of ravens rises & falls—
rises & falls—shimmering in the distance,
through heat waves in the air.

We hold hands & trip over broken sidewalks.
In front of the Playhouse, we're not speaking,
but not looking anywhere except at each other.
I think you might kiss me.

Every moment together has led to this one,
an important moment
that should lead
to other moments,
bigger moments,
each moment
more clarifying
than the last.

But hope is a flightless thing.

The clouds shift, & so does the light.
The day comes to an end,
& then it finds night.

You've married
a woman who isn't me.

Reality has become
this blossoming of a cactus
between my ribs.

3.

As night moves its limbs
through the land, you send me the address
of a hotel in Hialeah. You send me the room
number. You send me a time.

I can't keep answering
your call. You are not the direction
I need to head towards.

I hold on to you
in that hotel room, like old times,
your body burning like red coal
against my thighs. I want you
to take me by the jaw
(your kiss—brutal, consuming).
Pin your knees into
mine. Push hard against me.

I want hours later
to feel two sore spots
like crab apples
where you worked your hips
against my skin.

I am no longer a woman
of sense & action.
My old self is dead now & gone,
dead & gone,
dead & gone now,
fallen impossibly.

In an animal way,
I still know you.
There's a wilderness
inside of me
that you have keyed.

4.

Your face is flushed,
your hair wild,
unbrushed, & your smile
makes me wonder /
makes me remember
why I feel so wrong.

I imagine your wife,
the image quick: an arm,
a bare breast, a triangle of limbs,
the curve of her hips.
She's leaning into
you, grabbing your arm,
giggling a bit.

Paint chips rain
from the ceiling,
dotting my brown slacks
with specks of white.
I want to die alone
in this hotel room,
listening to songs
about dangerous hearts,
about messages
stuffed in bottles
set to sea.

After you've gone,
I curl up in the bed
the way household pets

do after their owners leave,
to revel in the warmth left behind.

The room has a heartbeat
of its own,
pulsing with space.

5.

You have married a good woman
who loves you. Who isn't me.
She carries your name.

In the kitchen at home,
the good woman
you've married has made Moros y Cristianos.
She puts her fingers over yours
& your muscles tense with memory.
She ignores your looking away,
failing to understand,
baring her neck again to the world.

In the beginning
it wasn't like this. She & you
walked arm in arm, smelling of adventure,
murmuring to each other
so that no one could tell
if you were lovers or just friends.

"It's going to be a girl," she says.
In her body she is carrying
a new life you've built together.

Then there's a little scrunched-up face,
a tiny little nose,
fingers the size of caterpillars.

Thinking about it leaves
a tinny taste in my mouth,

makes me itchy. You're
waiting for me to say something,
your face half-light, half-dark,
mottled with shadow,
the face of a stranger
trying to figure out who
I am, & why
I'm in that hotel room.

6.

I find myself listening
so hard
to the quiet
in the room
that my ears
begin to hurt.
I wait
for the world to end,
& then it does, & ends
& ends again.

I know we cannot continue
with the catastrophic collision
of bones on heated Hialeah nights.
There has to be
more to all of this
besides bodies
bending to each other.

More than just moments
of forgetting
before the anguish
comes rushing in
like a loss.

The hotel room
suddenly feels small:
you are too close,
as you stare,
as I look away,

so close
we have to arch
our necks back
to prevent
our faces
from touching.

7.

I sit up late at night & want to call you.
But I know that no matter how hard
I try, I'm not going to change. I feel
fingernails scratch inside my sternum.
I sting with the need to claw you
out of my existence. Yes, I could wake you.

You hide in the corners
of my mind & appear when I think I'm alone
—tall, broody, soulful. I am empty, I am glass.
Among the passersby, I see your nose,
or a quick profile of your frame,
or a movement
or two
that make my chest pound
with the kind
of excitement that will wake one up
from any dream.

I could have been that woman,
beside you in the morning,
combing back
the curls against your forehead,
but I wouldn't be happy.
I'd still be rushing off to a hotel
to meet a man who isn't you.
Perhaps all this time,
I've just been rushing
out to meet myself,
with a sullen introduction.

But I can't be contained
between sweat-soaked sheets.

Article XVI

I Will Practice Self-Talk

When depression brings
a chill that settles inside me,
a marrow-deep tremor,
when the impulse of fear
burns my palms, I'll tell
myself stories
about the village of my youth,
where days were sunny & mild,
the skies a cheerful,
eggshell blue,
where the river shivered
bright rubble, & sisters
lured each other out
into the sunshine.
I'll describe out loud
the two-hour hike up a steep,
rocky mountain trail among the happy
fuchsia of bougainvillea;
the acacias that crossed their limbs
along the roads; the walls of jasmine,
their dark branches covered with
white corollas; the lady-of-night vines
opening their blue bells in the evening.
I will tell myself
that those sisters
climbed a mountain with their strong legs,

and that one pair of those legs
are mine.

Article XVII

I Will Save Myself with Stories

1.

I followed Mother in her garden.
She was in a sleeveless
shirt & the top was unbuttoned,
revealing the mysterious line
of her cleavage. Strands
of her hair escaped
her bandana; her shoes
were soiled & muddy.
As she pruned the roses
or ran her hands on the stems
& undersides of the tomato leaves,
she talked about my grandfather
in reverent tones.
She loved Pa Roger, loved the stories
he'd told her—about growing up in France
with his Mexican mother, & later moving
to New Orleans,
where men & women danced
their hips & feet to the drums,
while their lips
spilled laughter as brittle
& shrill as clinking glasses
where sugary moonshine flowed.
She told me
how her parents met in Port-au-Prince, after Pa Roger

arrived in Haiti to manage
the railroad company.
How my grandfather
fell in love with the young woman
selling movie tickets
at Paramount Theaters.
How Grandma Clara
wore a gray beret on top
a head full of black curls.
How her laughter ran
clear across the street.
How Pa Roger went over to find out her name,
tried to speak to her, but Grandma Clara
was not interested. She wasn't like other girls
who chewed their cuticles
& jiggled their legs
nervously.
She had a strangely straight mouth,
a determined jaw.

I was jealous of this uncomplicated
love Mother felt for her own parents.
Her childhood was my phantom limb,
the thing once flesh, now gone
but living as a restless pricking under my skin.

2.

Later, I became a storyteller,
a ghost made into temporary flesh
by my passion
for the smell of books:
musty, inky—earthy, perhaps.
It wasn't just the smell of paper.
It was the sweat
of turning pages
to reach the next cliff,
the spilled coffee or hot chocolate,
hastily swabbed off
the pages of my mother's novels.
The smell of eagerness & the hunger
for words, like Sunday dinner,
roasting when your stomach is empty.
When I stumbled into
my tales, my sister crouched
on her knees in anticipation. It was not
the story so much as afternoon sounds
lapping at open curtains,
the room alive—the house sighed
& shuddered, breathing inaudibly
through its doors & windows.
The mosquito coils kept most
of the bugs away,
but once in awhile, a hand slapped
a calf or waved around a neck
to swish away the fierce, hungry buzzing.
I began the tale & Estrella fell into it.
She leaned in for certain parts, sweaty

sunburnt face, half-lit & half-dark,
mottled with shadow. She wriggled
back through other parts.
My voice deepened, & so did the story.
The words came from somewhere bigger than me
—they vibrated through the room,
wrapped in something ethereal that seemed
to convince my audience
it wasn't me speaking at all, but the evil
character in the story, the man
in the yellow raincoat. Estrella sat
with her knees up, holding her toes,
as we traveled lands of giant
moon creatures
& thirsty shapeshifters.

3.

Without stories, silence chewed me & swallowed
& I was suspended in the dark warmth
of its throat. Stories allowed me to skirt
the cutting edge of the world around me.
My life became a deconstructed text,
& I was surrounded by words
—their sustaining luxury & danger.
I fell into tales as if into a well,
where every breath was a story.
Sometimes ideas rushed like torrents,
poured like rain, saturated,
seeped, set, washed away my mind.
At other times,
my thoughts only quivered,
like air full of dragonflies,
shuddering all ways, here to there,
everywhere, yet nowhere
—they sparked like fireflies
& twinkled away.
The smoke of mosquito
coils curled in the air.
The mosquitoes
still whined,
a piercing whirr
close to my ear.

4.

There's a pain in the world
that follows people
like their shadow,
despite reason
and proportion.
But stories,
even sad ones,
keep the darkness
from wrapping us
in its long, barbed sleeves.
They spin us out
and back into their embrace.
We glide in their magic,
beaming, breathless
—forgetting what worries we have.

Article XVIII

I Will Remember to Breathe

I'll remember to breathe in the homeroom,
when my students slam their books down
& press chewed gum to the underside
of desks. Chairs squeak & books tumble
onto the floor, the pages
curling with use
as though they are burning
slowly. The overhead fluorescents
buzz to life,
& the room fills
with a shaky, friable light.
I'll remember my own school days.

On Wednesdays,
before lunch, we took Scripture Class
from Sister Claudette,
who brushed the wimple back
off her shoulder
as if it were a fall of long hair.
She told us Bible stories.
We prayed & held hands
& sang Jean-Claude Gianadda songs. We
clapped.
We hopped up
& down. When the bell rang
for recess, girls in blue jumpers

with white blouses
spilled into the halls,
yelling across the throngs
to each other
shouting out after a deep breath,

I'll remember to breathe at church
when the priest
lights the incense
& the altar boy rings a chime.
Gray smoke will curl up,
& fumes fill the room
with an acrid, intoxicating odor.
I will breathe in
the heavy smell
of incense that
stings my throat
& mouth already dry
from drinking
Manischewitz.
During the prayer, my hands
will swap sweat with other hands,
slip, clutch,
connect to something profound,
a source of stability, permanence,
transcendence.

I'll remember to breathe as unexpected
rain pummels palm trees
in the church garden,
the concrete walls,
the tiled roof. When the infidel wind
blows in through the edges
of the doors. I'll remember
to breathe as the sun slips
its last light
through the branches
of the coconut trees,
a disorienting, dusty light of gloomy
shivers,
illuminating the mahogany of kneeling
benches & cracks on the altar.

After mass, I'll remember to breathe
in the kind of heat that makes sleeping
next to a husband absurd,
the pulling apart
of skin, moist & elastic. I'll look
into the stutters & twitches
of his sleep, arms
in disarray like fish
confused by waves. His body
flinches, & clicks as he dreams,
the flickering of his eyelids
like moths that slow
their flight before landing.
In bed, we press
together,
my head pillowed
by a length of arm,
I listen to his breathing
—each inhale's up-strum.

I'll breathe so furiously
I won't be absorbed
in the unraveling
of promises I've made, & the anxiety
of being too much or not enough.

Article XIX

I Will Practice Gratitude

Gratitude magnifies the smallest things
—a thin wind across a wire, a single leaf
in unsuspecting light, star-shaped,
with a pointed lobe, swaying.

Gratitude poeticizes the waking sun,
a squint of sound, a flutter on a branch,
the lanky ibis with its heavy, long bill.
Clouds of shimmering butterflies
feed on black-eyed susans, & light glows
from inside the trees, spilling
from the leaves as the sun rises,
a rich, gold-tinted green.

Gratitude can save the world from its pain.

At the market in Hialeah, I'm grateful
for the soft air, the breeze of sweet
roasting coffee, the clouds in the sky
moving like fishing boats out
on the Caribbean Sea. The voices
of the neighborhood rise & fall
in spurts. The sun pacing the lighted sky
is warm on my neck. People mill about
on the streets, lips moving, probably chatting
about weekend plans

& the rest of their lives.

Others ride bicycles, young men
in crisp shirts, & women, curvy,
without makeup, wearing flowered dresses
in heat-slowed bodies.
A guitar player performs on the sidewalk
outside a coffee shop;
two men drink Inca Cola
in front of a bookstore.

Today, the shadows
have tilted
      away,
           away.

Dust blows along the pavement,
& heat
waves bounce
off parked cars
with curling bumper

stickers.
A bare-chested man drills
a jackhammer
into the asphalt,
his skin pouring sweat.
The road chokes
with foot traffic & vehicles.
Well into the afternoon,
the sun-wrinkled
women on the side of the road
sell homemade
peanut brittle,
piles of peppers,
tomatoes, mangoes,
& watermelons
stacked in pyramids on empty bags.
They leave before
thick fog envelops Calle Ocho,
before
giant drops ricochet off the hoods
& splatter the windshields
of cars that summon the worst from us
with their roar,
their violent, rattling basses. My head
jerks around quickly,
bones in my neck pop.

I'll be grateful despite the commotion.
Good or bad: today is my day.
No one else's.
When the sun rests its head
on the pillow of the horizon,
the bowl of the sky
fills with dark blue.
Palms trees creak against
the breeze that blows
the scent of night crawlers
& lady-of-the-night; their fronds rub against
each other as though whispering secrets.
I'll be grateful for the moon;
she settles a silvery
blanket of light over the city. Rats
squeak & rustle among the dry
weeds as the root for the ambrosia
of empty coconuts.
Coqui frogs sing their love-croaks
& I'm grateful for bougainvillea flowers
& the smell of rotting
breadfruit on the night air.

Article XX

I Will Practice Self-Care

It starts with a lightness in the stomach,
my body, empty on the inside.
Coolness passes over my heart
& wraps around it in a perplexing fashion.
I know this feeling for what it was—
my cushion of control is eroding,
& I am scared sleepless of what
will be revealed in its absence.
The moon is throwing knives
through the trees, I think,
looking up at the sky. & I know
it's time to hide from the world
& unfold inward—shape images
& emotions into structured plots.
I'm no longer a daughter, nor
a sister, nor a wife, nor a friend. I
no longer keep a part of myself
hidden away. I'm no longer a secret
waiting to reveal itself. I'm instead
a true tale unwinding

& I will love that.

Article XXI

I Will Remember to Self-Soothe

1.

Outside, in the night, where birds
lie huddled, slow-hearted, against one another,
the trees are dark & shapeless, & little girls,
they're afraid of everything. They don't yet know
that the shadows trailing behind them
are also a part of who they are.
Come here, child, I'll comfort you
like no one else can.

2.

Outside, in the night, where birds
lie huddled, slow-hearted, against one another,
the trees are dark & shapeless, & I,
I'm afraid of everything. I don't yet know
that the shadows trailing behind me
are also a part of what I am.
Come here, child, I'll comfort myself
like no one else can.

Article XXII

I'll Acknowledge That I Don't Know Which Way the Road Goes

FOR ANTON CERMAK

I was five when I knew
I would not die.
I walked out in a noiseless hour,
before dawn,
& listened to my breath
engulfed in silence
like Bayfront Park before the rustles
of traffic from the boulevard,
before the sirens in the distance,
even before the crows clink
against the curb, purring
& clicking
as they beak & throat the worms—
a silence so quiet, I heard nothing
but the sound
of an immeasurable thing
having nothing to do with me.

I refused the idea that I could vanish,
like rungs
of a ladder tugged out.
In the dark, I thought of a word,
then of another word, & I imagined
a sentence stretching
long enough, breaking
into a road that led
to where the dead ones roamed.

Here, in Bayfront Park,
in a noiseless hour, before dawn,
the real world falls away around me,
but the dead are rescued from oblivion
& turned into words,
into sentences,
into the plunges & loops
of handwriting.

Anton Cermak returns, alive,
a warm wind blowing
down the throat
of his suit in that afternoon in 1933,
ghosts quickening
on his every side.
He, who cannot hear,
listens for the cheering at the rally.
He, who cannot see,
watches President Roosevelt emerge
from a yacht after a fishing trip to the Bahamas.
He, who cannot smell,
inhales the gun's sharp glare.
He, who cannot feel, suffers again
the sudden burn of the two shots.
He sags, & his eyes are still black
—only the way out is closed.

Anton's plaque is shining & smooth
& I trace one word,
then another word,
& I imagine that they keep him
from disappearing,
so that it counts for something—
the handshake with the president,
the vigor of joy
in the hands
that clapped together,
the blouses heavy with Miami sweat,
the hot wind, the bullets,
the meaty hand on his shoulder,
the ride to Jackson Hospital.

What part of this is least terrifying?

It's easy to die.
It's the easiest thing we can do.
As people laugh & bikes speed past,
I take Anton's memory as a gift,
believing we can all cross
back over to this world,
wishing one another good night,
arranging play dates,
& returning to our cars.

One is a world of ghosts, & the other of the living,
but can you be certain which way the road goes?

Article XXIII

I Will Embrace Miami

I've been to plenty of places
I'd rather not have been.
Only in Miami am I not
tough & bitter like uncooked roots.

For me, Miami is the beat
of Haitian drums that become
hands on my hips, so that I forget
about gravity.
Miami is Barbancourt breath
It's the smell
of desert roses & begonias brilliant
beneath moon glow, of Caribbean
cigars & cigarettes, & of codfish.

Miami is a conspiracy of ravens
on telephone poles. Miami is roads
always under construction
& mud pools
that reflect stars.
Miami is mosquitoes
& sudden rain
after the sky is briefly gold.
It's the wind blowing in
onomatopoeias: howls
with no beginning.

Miami is botanicas & incantations
to the ancestral loas. It's Libreri Mapou
& its book festival. It's poetry flash
mobs, Haitian Flag Day, & the chicken
busters of Overtown.
In Miami, Port-au-Prince & Okap
seem so close, while Key West,
Pompano, & Homestead sound
like foreign lands.
Only in Miami does my chest
never sing its broad thrum of loneliness.
In Miami, my voice is not
the only one that rushes past pauses
& disregards emphasis. Almost
everyone's accent is slanted east,
vowels & consonants temperamental
& warm like Caribbean roads. I
find something inside myself,
asleep for so very long,
I don't know the word for it.

I've been to plenty of places
I'd rather not have been.
Only in Miami
am I a livewire flicking like a dare.

Above the treetops,
the sky is a bowl of stars
& the moon hangs low

Wild constellations
a sky rimmed in tangerine

tiny flecks of light

The night air, alive
with particles of water,
vibrates with birdsong.

Birds sing the coda
of their delirious night song.
Adieu. Oh, adieu.

It's a hazy dawn
with fat & dark thunderclouds,
murky, tadpole light

Article XXIV

I Will Allow Myself to Splurge

What I want right now
is to gorge
on foil-wrapped confections
shaped like zoo creatures.
Chocolate animals
will be skinned
& ravaged
On the Miami Metrorail,
in lines at the bank, at Cinépolis,
or at the Greenstreet Café,
I daydream of Latin pastelitos
& Bahamian guava duffs.
Wait 'til you see me,
jelly between my fingers,
frosting on my face.
I'm totally unglued.

Article XXV

I Will Ask for Help

When fog drifts through my mind,
the shapes of my thoughts,
obscure & distorted,
when a lead
weight settles in my stomach
& strains my breath,
the white of my eyes catch
& reflect the light,
I will ask for help—to reach into myself,
tame the beast inside me.
My house has a heartbreak
of its own,
pulsing with space,
waiting for me
to take one stand
or another:
live or die.

I will ask for help.

First,
I will try to take deep breaths.
If that doesn't
work, if the rage
burns deeper in the pit
of my stomach,
if each breath ignites the flame
brighter, if my bones
feel like they are disintegrating,
leaving my legs wobbly & weak,

I will ask for help.

Because there is no such thing
as jumping out of my skin to run.

I will ask for help.

Because the night can be
beautiful—full of damp
earth & the high calls
of nighthawks.

I will ask for help

to allow
my bitterness its exit, to vent hatred
& let it drift from the window
into the dark.

Article XXVI

I Will Keep the Faith

1.

In a church garden in Hialeah,
the limbs of the banyan trees
scrape across my face,
the hammock familiar in its mesh of branches
interwoven to form their own language.
You are here. Nowhere else. & you are divine.
I listen for the crush & the uncrush of my heart muscle.

It's Lent. From under the trees in their own quiet magic,
I hear the sermon of the priest inside the small church.
My lips move to words & prayers & benediction,
& I vow to persevere on the path to enlightenment,
until the kingdom,
until the power & the glory,
until the amen.

But I know the real world
will enter me again on Calle Ocho
(the turns, the honking, the restaurant signs!)
& breathe away my soul. Slowly, slowly—
& still no time to get out of the way.
On the Palmetto, no compass, no north.
I'll move even closer to the square root of nothing—
away from that something
beautiful & unknowable.

When I emerge from the church's garden
in the late Wednesday afternoon,
the air is deep clutched in my chest.
In the front yard, a man, his face pitted with shadows,
is selling mandarin oranges.
My sister is taking a picture
of the pink laurels with an iPhone.
She suggests dinner at El Rinconcito,
& I feel crackly in my veins,
as I imagine mouths that taste like chicken fricassée.
Oh, how little it takes to embrace the mundane.

2.

I've said to myself,
'There is no God,"
but my body objects.
My body knows truth
despite my brain.
In nature, I am dimmed
& distanced from the world
& its rumors. Closer
to something larger than myself,
something, I suppose,
others would call

God.

I lie in the moss of the bog
& watch the moon.
Why? The word barely a whisper
swallowed by wind,
a plea for something I can't have.
The air moves under its fragile weight.
Why? A knot of pain throbs
in the back of my neck.
I only return home
when the moon is high
above the trees,
laying a dust of light

over everything.

In the morning, the new light
will be clean, the air fresh,
the smell of late summer
moving across the lake,
the water cooler.

Acknowledgements

I want to thank Yaddyra Peralta and Jan Becker, editors nonpareil, and source of great support, great counsel, and encouragement. I am also indebted to the very patient Freesia McKee and Dariel Suarez who cheered me on to the finish line.

Thank you, Denise Duhamel and Campbell McGrath: You turned me into a poet!

Thank you, Edwidge Danticat, Allison Joseph, Scott Cunningham, Rich Ferguson, Jennifer Maritza McCauley, Anjanette Delgado, and Lorraine C. Ladish, for your support.

My gratitude to artist Danielle Boodoo-Fortuné and graphic designer Liz Hong for the beautiful cover of this book, and to Laura "Stella" Richardson for her guidance.

Thank you, Jenny Hearn and Katie Watkins.

Special thanks to Matthew Sharpe and Jesus David Felipe Bernal, whose suggestions and advice have been invaluable. Your feedback on the various drafts pushed me to be more honest to myself and to my readers. Special thanks to Donna Aza Weir-Soley for her careful comments and critiques of the entire manuscript, and Geoffrey Philp for using my poetic play as a teaching tool at Miami Dade College. I will never forget your kindness.

Thank you to the talented professionals who adapted earlier versions of this work for the theater, and directed the plays:

Rommel Arellan-Marinas (*No Pill for Loverhorn*, 2016); Gladys Ramirez (*If You're an Orange, I'm an Orange*, 2017); and Mahalia Solages (*Shadows of Hialeah*, 2016). Thank you, Jair Bula, Arturo Sierra, Chasity Hart, Charity Hannah Grace, and Guy-Marcel Lilavois Jr. for their artistic talent as they performed versions of Paloma and Jose Armando at the Miami MicroTheater, the O, Miami Festival's Poetry Press Week, and at the Compositum Musicae Novae's "Metamorphosis" event in Pinecrest Garden.

I also owe a debt of gratitude to my mother Carmita (who traveled from Haiti to surprise me at one of the performances), and to my sisters Patricia, Jennifer, and Nathalie who had faith in me and who encouraged me as a writer at a time when I needed it most. I love you.

Lots of love to my new family: Patricia Williams and Lisa Torchut, I love you.

I want to extend my appreciation to all the editors at Books & Books Press, an imprint of Mango Publishing. It's an inspiration to work with such a talented an giving group of people.

About the Author

Born in Port-au-Prince, Haiti, M.J. Fièvre currently writes from Miami.

M.J.'s publishing career began as a teenager in Haiti. Her first mystery novel, *Le Feu de la Vengeance*, was published at the age of sixteen. At nineteen, she signed her first book contract with Hachette-Deschamps, in Haiti, for the publication of a young adult book titled *La Statuette Maléfique*.
As of today, M.J. has authored nine books in French that are widely read in Europe and the French Antilles.

In the United States, One Moore Book released M.J.'s first children's book, *I Am Riding*, which is part of OMB's Haiti series edited by Edwidge Danticat. Beating Windward Press published M.J.'s memoir, *A Sky the Color of Chaos*, about her childhood in Haiti during the brutal regime of Jean-Bertrand

Aristide. M.J.'s short stories and poems in English have appeared in various anthologies, including *Flashes of Horror* (Horror Without Borders, 2019) and *Making Good Time* (Jai Alai Books, 2019), and her plays have been performed at the Miami MicroTheater and at the O, Miami Festival's Poetry Press Week.

M.J. earned a Bachelor's Degree in Education from Barry University and an MFA from the creative writing program at Florida International University. She taught writing for eight years at Nova Middle School in Davie and later became a writing professor at Broward College and Miami Dade College.

REWRITE
YOUR LIFE!
LEARN TO USE WRITING TO OVERCOME
ANXIETY, DEFEAT DEPRESSION, & GAIN
BOSS-LEVEL
CONFIDENCE.

WITH

M.J. FIEVRE

&

(OCCASIONALLY)

LOGAN

HAPPY, OKAY?

WWW.HAPPYOKAY.CLUB

Mango Publishing, established in 2014, publishes an eclectic list of books by diverse authors—both new and established voices—on topics ranging from business, personal growth, women's empowerment, LGBTQ studies, health, and spirituality to history, popular culture, time management, decluttering, lifestyle, mental wellness, aging, and sustainable living. We were recently named 2019's #1 fastest growing independent publisher by *Publishers Weekly*. Our success is driven by our main goal, which is to publish high quality books that will entertain readers as well as make a positive difference in their lives.

Our readers are our most important resource; we value your input, suggestions, and ideas. We'd love to hear from you—after all, we are publishing books for you!

Please stay in touch with us and follow us at:
Facebook: Mango Publishing
Twitter: @MangoPublishing
Instagram: @MangoPublishing
LinkedIn: Mango Publishing
Pinterest: Mango Publishing

Sign up for our newsletter at www.mango.bz and receive a free book!

Join us on Mango's journey to reinvent publishing, one book at a time.

CPSIA information can be obtained
at www.ICGtesting.com
Printed in the USA
BVHW080400010919
557329BV00001B/1/P

9 781642 501360